# Code Review Mastery

# Top Techniques and Resources for Excellent Code

Taylor Royce

# DEDICATION

To all the engineers and developers who never stop pushing the boundaries of quality, creativity, and perfection in their job. We are all inspired by your commitment to creating clear, effective code and enhancing the resources and procedures that help us in our work. This book is dedicated to you; I hope it will be a useful guide and resource for you as you traverse the always changing world of code review and development.

To my friends and family, who have been my pillar of support and encouragement throughout everything. Your admiration for my work inspires me to work hard and be persistent.

And to the innumerable peers, mentors, and coworkers who have shaped my career path in this industry by sharing their knowledge and thoughts. This work is a monument to the collective expertise and experience that we all share, and your contributions have been important.

# CONTENTS

# ACKNOWLEDGMENTS

To everyone who helped to finish this book, I would like to express my sincere gratitude. Throughout this journey, your assistance, knowledge, and encouragement have been priceless.

**To My Advisors and Associates:** I appreciate you sharing your knowledge and perspectives on the field of software development and code review. Your advice has molded my comprehension and substantially improved the precision and breadth of the information offered here.

**To My Friends and Family:** Your patience and steadfast support have been a source of strength. We appreciate your support over the long hours and your belief in the significance of our job.

**To the Engineers and Developers**: Your commitment to perfecting code review procedures and your passion for the craft of coding have always been an inspiration. The standards and innovations that you pursue on a daily basis are intended to be reflected in this book.

**To the Contributors and Reviewers**: Your comments and recommendations have been very helpful in honing and polishing this work. Thanks to your contributions, the content is now both applicable and useful to a wider range of developers.

**To the Groups and Companies**: I appreciate you sharing the difficulties and real-world background that shaped a lot of the case studies and examples in this book. Your willingness to share your experiences has enhanced and increased the applicability of the content.

**To the Audience:** The things that really make this book come to life are your involvement and interest in it. I hope the knowledge and perspectives I've provided will be helpful to you as you progress through the code review and software development process.

I sincerely thank each and every one of you for helping to make this project feasible.

## DISCLAIMER

The information in this book represents the author's knowledge and understanding at the time of writing and is only meant for general informational purposes. Although every attempt has been taken to guarantee the content's correctness and completeness, software development and code review are dynamic and ever-evolving fields. As a result, certain material might become old or might not be applicable in every circumstance.

Any errors or omissions in the content, as well as any actions based on the information in this book, are disclaimed by the author and publisher. The thoughts stated are the author's own and may not represent the beliefs or endorsements of any businesses, associations, or people that are mentioned.

When implementing the ideas and methods presented herein in their own work, readers are urged to use caution and consult experts. The information provided is not warranted or guaranteed to produce any particular result or benefit.

The use of this book or the information included within it may not result in any direct, indirect, incidental, or consequential damages at all from the author or publisher.

You accept and acknowledge these terms by reading this book.

# CHAPTER 1

## A Guide to Coding Review

## 1.1 What Does Code Review Mean?

## Concept and Objective of Code Review

The methodical analysis of software source code by developers who are not the code's original creator is known as code review. Its fundamental goal is to guarantee that the codebase stays error-free, clean, and manageable. Early in the development process, code reviews aid in spotting any problems like bugs, security flaws, or coding standards violations. Code reviews help promote shared knowledge and communal ownership of the codebase by encouraging team members to work together.

Code review is for more than just identifying mistakes. It acts as a learning aid, giving developers the helpful criticism they need to advance their abilities. In order to maintain uniformity throughout the codebase, code reviews also promote adherence to best practices and coding standards. The ultimate objectives are to raise the caliber of software, lower technical debt, and improve the development process as a whole.

## Advantages of Code Review for Organizations and Developers

**1. Improved Code Quality:** Before code is merged into the main branch, code reviews assist in identifying flaws and places for improvement, lowering the possibility of errors and issues in production.

**2. Knowledge Sharing:** Through peer review, developers can pick up new tricks, patterns, and best practices that advance team proficiency.

**3. Consistency:** Code reviews make sure that the codebase is consistent and maintainable, which is important for long-term projects. They also enforce coding standards and norms.

**4. Collaboration:** The procedure creates a cooperative atmosphere where team members talk through problems and find solutions as a group, strengthening the team dynamic.

**5. Reduced Technical Debt:** By identifying possible issues early on, technical debt can be avoided, which can ultimately save a substantial amount of time and money.

**6. Security:** To ensure that the code follows security best practices and shields the company from potential breaches, code evaluations frequently include checks for security vulnerabilities.

## Regular Obstacles in the Code Review Procedure

**1. Time Constraints:** Developers may experience pressure to complete code reviews quickly, which could result in the omission of important concerns. It's difficult to strike a balance between efficiency and thoroughness.

**2. Subjectivity:** Individual tastes may affect code reviews, resulting in inconsistent comments. Clearly defining rules and requirements can assist in lessening this difficulty.

**3. Resistance to Feedback:** During code reviews, developers who are sensitive to criticism may become resistant or defensive. Promoting a culture that values constructive criticism is crucial.

**4. Tooling Issues:** The procedure may become difficult and less efficient due to inadequate tools or poorly integrated code review systems. Purchasing the appropriate instruments is essential.

**5. Over-Reviewing:** Reviews that are overly thorough can impede the development process. The secret is striking the correct balance between efficiency and thoroughness.

**6. Knowledge Gaps:** Reviewers may provide irrelevant or inaccurate criticism because they may not completely comprehend the context or needs of the code they are evaluating. It is crucial to make sure reviewers have sufficient information.

## 1.2 The Procedure for Code Reviews

### Critical Steps in a Code Review

**1. Preparation:** The code writer sends in their modifications for approval, making sure the code is properly documented and follows coding guidelines. To aid reviewers in comprehending the goal and extent of the revisions, they might also include background information on the changes.

**2. Review:** Reviewers check the code for errors, correctness of design overall, and compliance with coding standards. This entails looking for logical mistakes, possible bugs, security holes, and optimization opportunities.

**3. Feedback:** Reviewers offer their input by highlighting problems, making suggestions for enhancements, and posing queries where more information is required. The criticism must be helpful and centered on enhancing the code.

**4. Discussion:** To elucidate criticism, settle disputes, and explore potential solutions, the author and reviewers converse. This is the critical phase in coming to an agreement on the required modifications.

**5. Revisions:** Based on the comments received, the author makes the required adjustments and, if necessary, submits the code again for review.

**6. Approval:** The code is accepted and included into the main branch after all problems have been fixed. This last stage certifies that the code satisfies the necessary quality requirements.

## Participants' roles and responsibilities

**1. Code Writer:** The programmer who composes the code

and sends it in for approval. They are in charge of making sure the code is prepared for review, giving background information, and implementing the required changes in response to criticism.

**2. Reviewer:** A developer, or group of developers, who check the code for errors, overall quality, and compliance with standards. Reviewers offer suggestions and assist the author in resolving any problems.

**3. Team Lead/Architect:** Occasionally, code that introduces major modifications or has an influence on the overall system design may be reviewed by a team lead or architect. They guarantee that the code complies with the long-term objectives and architectural guidelines of the project.

**4. Quality Assurance Engineer:** To make sure the code satisfies quality assurance requirements and does not introduce new defects or regressions, QA engineers may take part in code reviews in certain workflows.

**Optimal Methods for Efficient Code Review**

**1. Set Clear norms:** Specify rules and norms for coding that each team member is required to adhere to. This guarantees uniformity across the codebase and lessens subjectivity in reviews.

**2. Prioritize High-Risk Areas:** Pay close attention to code reviews that impact important application components, have security ramifications, or need intricate logic. High-risk locations should be prioritized to identify problems early.

**3. Limit the Scope:** Steer clear of sending huge changesets to reviewers. The review process is more focused and effective when modifications are broken down into smaller, more manageable chunks.

**4. Use solutions Effectively:** Make use of code review solutions that automate tedious tasks, connect with your development environment, and expedite the review procedure.

**5. Promote a Positive Culture:** Invite considerate and enlightening criticism. Understand that the purpose of code review is not to point fingers; rather, it is to enhance the team's abilities and the quality of the code.

**6. Promote Pair Programming:** By enabling two developers to work together on code in real-time, pair programming can enhance code reviews by minimizing the need for in-depth reviews down the road.

**7. Review Frequently:** Smaller, more frequent evaluations are more productive than larger, less frequent ones. Set up a code review schedule that corresponds with your development process.

**8. Document Learnings:** Establish a common knowledge base containing best practices, frequent problems, and insights from code reviews. The team as a whole can use this documentation as a reference.

## 1.3 Measures of Code Reviews

## Key Performance Indicators to Monitor for Code Review

**1. Review Coverage:** The proportion of code modifications that undergo evaluation. High coverage denotes in-depth reviews, whilst poor coverage can imply that certain changes are passing without much examination.

**2. Review Time:** How long does it typically take to finish a code review? Keeping an eye on this indicator makes sure that reviews are completed on time and assists in locating process bottlenecks.

**3. Defect Density:** The quantity of flaws discovered for every 100 lines of code, for example. Monitoring defect density facilitates evaluation of both the efficiency of the review process and the caliber of the code being written.

**4. Rework Ratio:** The percentage of the code that, following review, requires revision. When code is submitted for review and fails to meet quality standards, it may be indicated by a high rework ratio.

**5. Code Churn:** The rate of rewriting or refactoring code. Elevated code turnover may suggest instability within the codebase, maybe indicating problems with the design or review procedure.

## Method for Measuring the Effectiveness and Efficiency of Code Reviews

**1. Quantitative Metrics:** Keep track of metrics including the rework ratio, defect density, review coverage, and review time. These metrics offer a quantitative foundation for evaluating the efficacy and efficiency of the code review procedure.

**2. Qualitative Feedback:** Get developers' opinions about the code review procedure. Retrospectives and surveys can provide light on topics that quantitative measures would miss, like how helpful people think feedback is or how simple it is to work together on reviews.

**3. Comparison across Time:** To spot trends, compare measurements on a regular basis across time. For instance, a reduction in review time combined with a stable or improved defect density could be a sign of increasing efficiency in the review process.

**4. Correlation with Production Issues:** Examine how code review metrics and post-release issues relate to one another. A higher frequency of bugs discovered after deployment can mean that stricter code review procedures are required.

**Improving the Code Review Process with Metrics**

**1. Identify bottlenecks:** To pinpoint process delays, use indicators such as review time. Code reviews may be completed more quickly and effectively if certain bottlenecks are removed.

**2. Enhance Training:** Metrics that show a high rework ratio or low review coverage may point to the necessity of further instruction in either the review procedure or coding standards.

**3. Streamline Processes:** Metrics can be used to find places where the review procedure can be made more efficient. For instance, tighter review standards or better early design processes could be advantageous if code churn is high.

**4. Set Goals:** Set objectives for important metrics, including decreasing review times or raising defect detection percentages. The code review procedure can be continuously improved by examining these objectives on a regular basis.

**5. Support Best procedures:** Highlight and encourage the team to implement good review procedures by sharing metrics-driven insights. Acknowledging effective tactics can encourage a team-wide adoption of them.

# CHAPTER 2

## 2.1 Review of Over-the-Shoulder Code

### Scope and Procedure

An informal yet efficient technique called "over-the-shoulder" code review involves a developer typically the code author walking through their work with a team member or coworker. The author goes through each line of the code or talks about particular areas with the reviewer, who gives quick input, poses queries, or makes suggestions for improvement.

### The procedure is simple:

**1. Initiation:** A reviewer is invited by the code author to go over the code with them.

**2. Walkthrough:** The author explains the reasoning, intent, and usefulness of the code by either physically sitting next to the reviewer or by sharing their screen in a co-located environment.

**3. Real-time Feedback:** The reviewer points out possible problems, provides clarification, and makes immediate edits or enhancement suggestions.

**4. Revision:** Based on the input gathered throughout the session, the author may need to make quick revisions.

**Properties and Drawbacks**

**Benefits:**

- **Quick Response:** Over-the-shoulder evaluations are real-time, so questions can be answered right away and problems can be resolved quickly.
- **Efficiency:** Since this approach doesn't call for the use of special tools or the scheduling of meetings, it may be quicker than more formal code review procedures.
- **Collaboration:** It promotes open dialogue and teamwork among members, strengthening understanding and information exchange.
- **Contextual Understanding:** The reviewer provides more pertinent criticism as a result of having a better

grasp of the context of the code and the author's intentions.

## Disadvantages:

- **Limited Scope:** Due to their informal nature, over-the-shoulder assessments may overlook more significant flaws or fail to reveal more complex issues that call for closer inspection.
- **Disruption:** If the procedure is not prearranged, it may cause disruptions to the author's and reviewer's workflow.
- **Subjectivity:** Depending on the reviewer's background and tastes, the absence of uniform standards may result in reviews that are inconsistent.
- **Deficit in Records:** For tracking and auditing purposes, it can be problematic because there is frequently no record of the review process because the feedback is provided verbally and in real-time.

## Optimal Applications

- **little Code Modifications:** In situations where the influence on the codebase is negligible and prompt feedback is adequate, over-the-shoulder reviews are perfect for little, incremental modifications.

- **Learning and Mentorship:** In mentorship scenarios, when a senior developer can walk a junior developer through the code, this method is especially helpful.

- **Time-sensitive Situations:** This method can work very well when there is a pressing requirement to swiftly review and incorporate code.

- **Prototyping and Exploration:** This informal review approach works well for experimental code or prototypes when the goal is to explore ideas rather than produce production-ready code.

## 2.2 Working in Pairs

### Scope and Procedure

When two developers collaborate on the same piece of code at the same time, it's called pair programming. The "driver," one developer, creates the code, while the "navigator," the second developer, goes over each line of code as it is written. In real time, the navigator offers comments, makes suggestions for enhancements, and assists in spotting possible problems. To keep people interested and distribute the workload, the jobs are alternated on a regular basis.

**Usually, the procedure entails:**

**1. Preparation:** The couple decides on the work at hand, arranges the required space, and talks over their strategy.

**2. Active Coding:** While the navigator watches, checks, and gives prompt feedback, the driver develops the code and expresses their thought process.

**3. Role Switching:** To maintain a balanced workload and to keep both developers actively participating, the duo switches duties on a frequent basis.

**4. Continuous Review:** Throughout the session, the code is continuously examined and enhanced, eliminating the need for additional code reviews afterwards.

**Pros and Drawbacks**

**Advantages:**

- **Enhanced Code Quality:** Constant inspection by the navigator makes sure that best practices are adhered to right from the start and helps identify issues early.

- **Knowledge Sharing:** Pair programming is a great method for team members to exchange skills and knowledge, which promotes a cooperative learning environment.

- **Decreased Overhead for Code Review:** There is frequently less need for a separate code review procedure after the code is produced because the code is reviewed in real-time.

- **Enhanced Problem-Solving:** When two developers collaborate, they can approach issues from several perspectives, which results in more creative and reliable solutions.

- **Speedier Accrual:** By partnering with more seasoned developers, new team members can quickly become familiar with the codebase and development procedures.

**Difficulties:**

- **Resource-Intensive:** Pair programming necessitates the collaboration of two developers on a single task, perhaps resulting in less effective resource allocation.

- **Potential for Conflicts:** Disparities in viewpoints, coding preferences, or levels of expertise may cause disagreements or hostility between the two.

- **Fatigue:** Constant teamwork can be mentally taxing, particularly if there are extended stretches without breaks or if the developers are not a good fit.

- **Skill Mismatch:** If the two developers' skill levels are significantly different, the more seasoned developer may control the meeting and lessen the efficiency of the partnership.

## How to Effectively Use Pair Programming

**1. Make the Correct Pairs:** Assign developers with corresponding levels of expertise and skill. A balanced mix of knowledge is ideal for pairs so that each member may make a significant contribution.

**2. Set Clear Goals:** Prior to beginning, decide on the session's goals and parameters. This keeps the two on target and focused on the task at hand.

**3. Make a Schedule:** To keep both developers interested and avoid burnout, decide on regular intervals for role-switching. For instance, it's typical to replace every 30 to 60 minutes.

**4. Encourage Communication:** Open and constant communication is crucial to successful pair programming. Urge the navigator to make suggestions or ask questions, and encourage the driver to share their reasoning.

**5. Offer pauses:** To avoid weariness and preserve productivity, make sure that partners take regular pauses. Focus and mental clarity can both be enhanced by brief breaks.

**6. Rotate Pairs:** Changing up the pairings amongst team members on a regular basis can help diffuse knowledge and keep silos from forming.

## 2.3 Official Code Assessment

### Scope and Procedure

Formal code review is an organized, methodical method of evaluating code that usually calls for several reviewers and a clearly defined procedure. Formal code reviews, in contrast to informal approaches, are frequently tracked and documented, guaranteeing that comments and choices are noted for future use. Formal reviews can be carried out in a number of ways, including in-person meetings, specialized code review tools, and email exchanges.

**Typically, the procedure entails:**

**1. Code Submission:** Using a specialized tool that manages the submission and review process, the author uploads the code for review.

**2. Assignment of Reviewers:** Based on their experience, the intricacy of the code, and the project's implications, particular reviewers are allocated to the code.

**3. Review Phase:** Reviewers check the code for errors, correctness of design, compliance with coding guidelines, and other pertinent aspects. Emails or the review tool are both used to submit written feedback.

**4. Discussion and Resolution:** The reviewers and author talk over the criticism, work out any squabbles, and decide what has to be changed.

**5. Edits and Approval:** The writer makes the necessary adjustments and sends the code again. After every problem has been fixed, the code can be merged.

**6. Documentation:** All phases of the process, including final approval, modifications, and comments, are recorded. This paperwork acts as a record for audits and references in the future.

## Various Formal Code Review Techniques

**1. Email Reviews:** Using this method, reviewers are emailed the code, and they react with comments. Despite being straightforward, managing this approach can be difficult, particularly for large teams or codebases.

**2. Online platforms:** Code reviews can be submitted, reviewed, and tracked using specialized online platforms like GitHub, Bitbucket, or Gerrit. These tools offer features like inline comments, approval protocols, and metrics tracking, and they frequently interface with version control systems.

**3. In Person Consultations:** Moreover, code reviews might take place in formal meetings when the team presents and discusses the code. When implementing significant or sophisticated code changes that call for input from several stakeholders, this approach might be helpful.

## Value of Recordkeeping and Monitoring

**1. Accountability:** By ensuring that all choices and

comments are documented, formal documentation holds participants accountable for their involvement in the review process.

**2. Traceability:** Documentation leaves a transparent trail of the things that were examined, altered, and changed for what reason. This traceability is essential for future debugging and auditing as well as for comprehending the codebase's progress.

**3. Knowledge Sharing:** Written evaluations are a resource that the team as a whole can use to learn from the problems found and the fixes put in place.

**4. Continuous Improvement:** By keeping track of metrics and recording comments, teams may evaluate the success of their code review procedure and make informed decisions.

**5. Compliance:** Formal documentation of the code review process is frequently required in businesses where regulatory compliance is required. It proves that the company upholds strict code quality standards and adheres to best practices.

# CHAPTER 3

ESTABLISHING A CULTURE OF CODE REVIEWS

## 3.1 Fostering a Good Environment for Code Reviews

### Building a Collaborative and Learning Culture

Establishing an atmosphere that emphasizes cooperation and lifelong learning is the first step in developing a constructive code review culture. Developers that work in a collaborative environment are more likely to consider code reviews as a chance to exchange knowledge, hone skills, and improve the codebase as a whole rather than merely as a method of quality assurance. To do this, one must embrace code reviews as an essential component of professional development rather than seeing them as a chore to be finished.

- **Encourage Peer Learning:** Motivate developers to see code reviews as opportunities for mutual learning. Junior developers can provide new ideas and insights, and senior developers can impart knowledge and best practices. Everyone gains from this exchange, which also improves the team's overall performance.

- **Establish Constructive Criticism as Normal:** Create a standard where criticism is never given and is always directed toward progress. Feedback ought to be balanced, precise, and directed toward the code rather than the coder—highlighting both areas that need work and those that are done well.

- **Promote Mentoring:** Assign less seasoned developers to mentors who can help them navigate the process of code reviews. In addition to fostering the growth of skills, this strengthens interpersonal ties within the team.

## Promoting Feedback and Open Communication

The foundation of a successful code review culture is open communication. It guarantees that no team member has to worry about being judged when voicing opinions, posing queries, or offering criticism.

- **Sponsor Conversation:** Throughout the review process, invite reviewers to clarify any unclear points and talk about alternative strategies. The author and the critic should feel appreciated and heard in this two-way dialogue.

- **Encourage Transparency:** Provide transparency for the code review procedure. Each member of the team needs to be aware of the objectives, requirements, and standards surrounding code reviews. Openness fosters trust and guarantees that the procedure is regarded as just and advantageous.

- **Consistent Visits:** Call frequent team meetings to go over the code review procedure, exchange stories, and resolve any issues. This helps to spot any issues before they become problems and maintains open lines of communication.

## Resolving Disagreements and Conflicts

Any team environment will always experience conflicts and disputes, but how they are handled can have a big impact on the dynamics of the team as a whole and the efficiency of the code review process.

- **Set Up Guidelines:** Establish explicit guidelines for handling disagreements. This could involve protocols for polite discourse, reaching consensus, and determining when to report a problem when an agreement cannot be achieved.

- **Pay Attention to the Code, Not the Person:** Request that team members direct their criticism towards the code itself, not the person who wrote it. This makes the conversation objective and productive by excluding the involvement of personal feelings.

- **Appoint a Mediator:** When a conflict becomes more intense or cannot be settled amicably, assign a senior team member or an impartial third party to mediate. This individual can assist in facilitating a resolution by offering an unbiased viewpoint and making sure the discussion stays constructive.

## 3.2 Formulating Standards for Code Reviews

## Outlining Detailed Code Quality Requirements

Code reviews must adhere to precise, well-defined code quality criteria in order to be efficient and reliable. As a guide for all code submissions, these standards ought to represent the team's principles, technical specifications, and industry best practices.

- **Requirements for Documents:** Make a thorough document outlining the rules for code quality that the team has agreed upon. Coding conventions (such as naming conventions, formatting, and indentation) and more sophisticated issues like code architecture, performance, and security should all be covered in this article.

- **Update Often:** In order to take into account new

knowledge, methods, and technologies, the standards should be routinely evaluated and updated. Updating the standards makes sure that the code review procedure is still applicable and efficient.

- **Make Standards Accessible:** Ascertain that every team member has easy access to the code quality standards. This might be accomplished by integration with the group's code review tools, a shared document, or an internal wiki.

## Establishing Participants' Expectations

All parties involved in the code review process should have clear expectations, since this will guarantee that everyone knows their roles and duties and that the workflow is streamlined.

- **Assignments to Reviewers:** Specify the expectations for reviewers, such as the scope of the review, the areas of emphasis, and the due dates for response. Reviewers ought to be in charge of verifying, for instance, that the code is correct and that it follows quality standards, is readable, and does not have any negative effects on the system as a whole.

- **Writer Accountabilities:** In a similar vein, before sending code for review, authors should be aware of what is anticipated. This involves making certain that their code is thoroughly tested, adheres to the standards of the team, and is properly documented. Additionally, authors need to be ready to talk about their code and quickly address criticism.

- **Timeliness:** Establish precise deadlines for the duration of reviews. Giving reviewers enough time to carefully go over the code is crucial, but it's just as critical to prevent bottlenecks that impede development. Setting realistic timelines aids in maintaining the process's efficiency.

## Developing a Checklist for Code Reviews

A useful instrument that guarantees uniformity and comprehensiveness in the review procedure is a code review checklist. It gives reviewers an organized method to follow, assisting them in concentrating on important facets of the code.

- **Fundamentals:** Add necessary components to the checklist, like following code guidelines, logic consistency, testing coverage, performance concerns, and security implications. These components must be customized to the unique requirements and goals of the team.

- **Personalized Checklists:** Give the checklist some leeway so that it can be modified to fit various kinds of code reviews. For example, a frontend code review checklist may be different from a backend services checklist.

- **Automated Integration:** Incorporate the checklist into the team's code review instruments as much as feasible. By automatically highlighting checklist items for reviewers as they walk through the code, this can expedite the process.

# 3.3 Ongoing Enhancement

## Collecting Input from the Group

To ensure that the code review process is continuously improved, it is essential to routinely get team feedback. Both the procedure and the participants' experiences should be covered in this feedback.

- **Unidentified Surveys:** Conduct anonymous surveys on a regular basis to get team members' honest opinions about the code review procedure. Questions might address the value of feedback, the effectiveness of the procedure, and any difficulties encountered.

- **Discussions Open:** In team meetings, promote candid conversations regarding the code review procedure. Establish a safe environment where team members may express their ideas and recommendations for enhancement without worrying about facing consequences.

- **Actionable Insights:** Examine the comments to see patterns, reoccurring problems, and opportunities for development. The intention is to use this data to improve the efficiency and enjoyment of the code review process for all parties involved.

## Examining Data from Code Reviews

One effective method for enhancing the code review procedure is data analysis. Teams may learn how the process is working and where it needs to be improved by monitoring and evaluating important KPIs.

- **Primary Measures:** Keep track of critical data including the number of comments per review, the length of time it takes to review a piece of code, and the frequency of code faults found during reviews. These indicators can be used to identify areas of concern, bottlenecks, and potential process simplification opportunities.

- **A Study of Trends:** Examine the data over time for patterns. For instance, if review times are steadily rising, this can mean that the team is getting too busy or that the codebase is getting more complex. The team may proactively resolve problems before they have an impact on production by being aware of these tendencies.

- **Analytical Information:** Think about qualitative information as well, such as the substance and tone of review comments, in addition to quantitative measurements. This can reveal information about the standard of feedback being offered and the general communication health of the team.

## Implementing Modifications to Enhance the Procedure

Not only must opportunities for improvement be identified, but concrete efforts must also be taken to implement improvements that improve the code review process in order to engage in continuous improvement.

- **Pilot Modifications:** Before implementing new procedures or resources for the full team, think about testing them out on a smaller group of people. This reduces disturbance and permits modifications in response to preliminary input.

- **Iterative Approach:** When improving processes, take an iterative approach. Large-scale overhauls are frequently more disruptive and difficult to manage than small, incremental adjustments. Evaluate these changes' effects on a regular basis and make necessary adjustments.

- **Record and Disseminate:** Make sure that any modifications to the code review procedure are properly recorded and shared with the team. By doing this, you can make sure that everyone is aware of the new procedures and expectations and is on the same page.

Teams can greatly increase the effectiveness of their code reviews by committing to continuous improvement, creating clear criteria, and cultivating a positive code review culture. This enhances the codebase's quality and promotes a more cooperative, encouraging, and fruitful work environment.

# CHAPTER 4

## 4.1 Crucial Elements of a Coding Review Instrument

## Key Features for Efficient Code Review

To improve productivity and expedite the review process, effective code review solutions need to provide a core set of features. These features guarantee code quality and facilitate effective collaboration between writers and reviewers.

- **Code Equivalency:** The ability to compare various code versions is a basic component of any code review tool. This features visual diffs, which make it simpler to identify additions, deletions, and revisions by highlighting changes across versions.

- **Comments inline** Reviewers can offer comments

straight within the code via inline commenting. This feature makes sure that comments are linked to particular lines or code segments, giving feedback that is both explicit and context-specific.

- **Review state Tracking:** Tools ought to provide the ability to monitor the state of code reviews, including those that are pending, ongoing, and finished. This guarantees that evaluations are finished on time and aids in workflow management.

- **Approval Mechanism**: Reviewers can accept or reject code changes through an approval system. Enforcing code quality standards and making sure all work satisfies team requirements prior to merging depend heavily on this method.

**Version Control System Integration**

Code review tools are made more effective when they are integrated with version control systems (VCS). The integration guarantees smooth cooperation and upholds consistency between code modifications and review procedures.

- **Synchronous Syncing:** The tool needs to automatically update review statuses and import code changes by syncing with the VCS. This guarantees that reviewers are constantly working with the most recent version of the code and minimizes manual labor.

- **Management of the Branch:** The program can manage pull requests and code reviews for many branches thanks to integration with VCS. In order to coordinate with continuous integration workflows and manage code reviews in a multi-branch development environment, this capability is required.

- **Commit History Access:** Reviewers should be able to read earlier revisions and comprehend the background of the current review by having access to the commit history through review tools. This aids in determining the effects of code modifications and guarantees continuity with the project's past.

## Features of Collaboration and Communication

Throughout the code review process, it is crucial to have effective collaboration and communication elements in place to facilitate discussions and resolve problems.

- **Threads for Discussion:** In order to facilitate discussions between writers and reviewers regarding particular edits or remarks, the tool ought to enable threaded discussions. This feature makes sure that all pertinent topics are covered and keeps debates structured.

- **Notifications and Alerts:** Participants receive automated notifications and alerts when there are new comments, status updates for reviews, or impending actions. By doing this, it is made sure that authors and reviewers are aware and able to react quickly to requests or criticism.

- **Feed of Activity:** An activity feed gives a summary of the most current updates and actions pertaining to code reviews. Team members can detect any unresolved concerns and stay informed about the status of reviews with the help of this tool.

## 4.2 Selecting the Appropriate Code Review Instrument

## Aspects to Take Into Account While Choosing a Tool

Selecting the best code review tool requires weighing a number of considerations to make sure it fits the goals of the team and works well with current processes.

- **Team Size and Structure:** Take into account your team's composition and size. Smaller teams might benefit from more straightforward solutions, but larger teams or geographically dispersed teams might need systems with sophisticated collaboration features.

- **Needs for Integration:** Evaluate the tool's compatibility with your current development tools and processes, such as project management software, continuous integration pipelines, and version control systems.

- **Customization and Scalability:** Assess the tool's ability to be tailored to your team's unique workflows and its capacity to expand with your projects or team as they expand.

## Assessment Standards for Various Tool Categories

Code review tools come in several varieties, each with unique features and functionalities. Finding the ideal tool for your needs is made easier by evaluating these ones according to predetermined standards.

- **Application:** Examine the features that various tools provide, including as review tracking, code comparison, and comment management. Make sure the tool has the features your code review process requires.

- **Usability:** Take into account the user interface and usability. An interface that is easy to use and provides clear navigation can increase adoption rates and streamline the code review process.

- **Support and Documentation:** Assess the degree of assistance and records offered by the tool supplier. The implementation process can be streamlined and problems can be resolved with the use of thorough documentation, tutorials, and prompt support.

## Benefit-Cost Analysis

To ascertain whether purchasing a code review tool will benefit your team and company, do a cost-benefit analysis.

- **Starting Expenses:** Consider the upfront costs associated with buying or licensing the instrument. Take into account any additional setup, integration, and customization costs.

- **Ongoing Costs:** Take into account recurring expenses including maintenance, subscription fees, and prospective upgrades. Make sure that these expenses line up with your long-term goals and budget.

- **Improved Return on Capital:** Analyze the tool's potential return on investment (ROI) by taking into account its advantages, which include better code quality, quicker review times, and increased teamwork. To calculate overall worth, weigh these advantages over the expenses.

## 4.3 Code Review Tool Implementation

### Introducing the New Tool to Developers

Effective onboarding is necessary for the successful installation of a new code review tool in order to guarantee that all team members feel at ease using it.

- **Overview and Introduction:** To acquaint the team with the capabilities, advantages, and ways in which the tool fits into current processes, conduct an introduction workshop. The goal of the tool, its main features, and how it will improve the code review procedure should all be covered in this session.

- **Hands-On Training:** Provide developers with opportunities to practice tool usage in a supervised setting by offering hands-on training sessions. Team members' confidence is bolstered by this hands-on experience, which also guarantees that they feel at ease using the tool.

- **References and Documentation:** Offer thorough resources and documentation, including FAQs, user manuals, and video tutorials. Developers can use these resources as a reference when they first use the tool, and they should be freely available.

## Resources for Training and Assistance

To get the most out of the code review tool and take care of any problems that may come up, ongoing training and support are crucial.

- **Consistent Training Sessions:** Arrange for regular training sessions to go over advanced features, fresh upgrades, or typical problems. Frequent training guarantees that the team stays current and continues to use the technology efficiently.

- **Resources for Support:** Provide a support system so that team members can contact you if they run into problems using the tool. This can be a specialized support group, in-house specialists, or a question-and-answer forum.

- **Feedback Mechanism:** Provide a way for users to provide feedback on their experiences using the tool. Utilize these comments to pinpoint areas that need work and to modify the tool or the way it's used.

## Optimal Methods for Adopting Tools

It is necessary to adhere to best practices when implementing a new code review tool in order to guarantee seamless integration and efficient use.

- **Gradual Rollout:** Take into account introducing the tool to the team gradually, first including a pilot group and then the complete group. This method ensures a more seamless transition by enabling troubleshooting and modifications based on early input.

- **Support Adoption:** Highlight the advantages of the tool to persuade team members to use it. Emphasize achievements, communicate successful results, and address any worries or opposition to change.

- **Monitor and Adjust:** Constantly keep an eye on how the tool is being used and solicit user input. Prepare to make changes in response to this feedback in order to resolve any problems and improve the tool's overall efficacy.

Through comprehension of the fundamental characteristics of code review instruments, assessment of alternatives according to crucial elements, and proficient application of the tool, groups can greatly improve their code review procedures. This fosters a more effective and productive development environment in addition to enhancing code quality and teamwork.

# CHAPTER 5

WELL-LIKED TOOLS FOR CODE REVIEW

## 5.1 Tools for Git-Based Code Reviews

### Git-Based Tools Overview

Git version control systems and Git-based code review tools combine to offer smooth code review procedures inside well-known Git platforms. These tools provide a number of features intended to help with code quality assurance and collaboration right within the Git environment.

## Features:

- **GitHub:** The code review features of GitHub, such as pull requests, inline comments, and code suggestions, are well known. It includes comprehensive review histories, connects with continuous integration (CI) technologies, and supports automatic merging.

- **Process:** Pull requests are created by developers to suggest changes, and team members review them. Reviewers have the option to accept or reject the pull request, make revisions requests, and comment on individual lines of code. The changes are merged into the main branch after they are accepted.

- **Advantages:** GitHub works with a wide variety of third-party tools and is easy to use. Further extensions and connections are available through its vast community and marketplace.

- **Deficits:** Teams utilizing alternative version control systems may find their options limited by GitHub's tight integration with its platform regarding review tools. In addition, compared to subscription programs, its free tier offers fewer features.

**Features:**

- **GitLab:** GitLab offers comprehensive code review capabilities, such as code quality checks, merge requests, and inline conversations. In addition, it offers capabilities like code analytics and security scanning and connects CI/CD pipelines.

- **Process:** Developers create merge requests for code reviews, just like on GitHub. Reviewers have the option to accept or reject merge requests, make changes, and offer comments. The CI/CD tools' connection with GitLab automates deployment and testing.

- **Advantages:** GitLab's feature-rich feature set supports end-to-end DevOps methods, and its integrated CI/CD capabilities expedite the development workflow.

- **Deficits:** GitLab's self-hosted version may need a lot of upkeep and setting, and its vast feature set may make the platform confusing for novice users.

**Features:**

- **Bitbucket:** Bitbucket provides branch permissions, inline commenting, and pull requests with inline comments. It is compatible with all of Atlassian's products, including Jira, which is used for problem tracking.

- **Workflow:** Team members debate and approve pull requests that developers submit for review. Bitbucket facilitates interaction with Atlassian's CI/CD technologies and allows automated testing.

- **Advantages:** The way Bitbucket integrates with Jira and other Atlassian technologies improves problem tracking and project management. Additionally, it supports the version control systems Mercurial and Git.

- **Deficits:** Compared to GitHub and GitLab, Bitbucket's user interface may be less straightforward, and its feature set might not be as comprehensive at the free tier.

## Workflow and Features of Code Reviews

- **Pull/Merge Requests:** An essential component of the Git-based review process, pull or merge requests let developers suggest changes for evaluation and discussion by the team. This helps with code reviews.

- **Inline Comments:** Reviewers are able to directly comment on individual lines of code, providing concise and context-specific input.

- **Approval Mechanisms:** These tools give reviewers the ability to accept or reject modifications, making sure that only code that has been examined and approved is combined.

- **Automated Testing:** Code changes can be automatically tested by integrating with continuous integration systems, which gives quick feedback on possible problems.

## Advantages and Drawbacks

- **Advantages:** Git-based solutions provide a variety of integrations with different development tools, broad collaboration options, and a smooth interaction with Git. Teams who already use Git for version control will find them ideal.
- **Weaknesses:** Because of their large feature sets, they can occasionally have a steep learning curve and provide less flexibility for teams utilizing other version control systems.

## 5.2 Independent Code Review Instruments

## Well-liked Independent Choices

Code review technologies that function apart from version control systems provide certain functionalities that are exclusive to code review.

## Features:

**Review Board:** Git, Subversion, and Perforce are just a few of the version control systems that Review Board supports for code review. It provides code diffs, inline comments, and bug tracking system integration.

- **Features:** With features specifically designed for review procedures, like comprehensive review dashboards and adaptable review workflows, Review Board offers a dedicated code review environment.

- **Equation using Tools Based on Git:** Review Board is a flexible choice for teams utilizing various version control systems since it places less emphasis on version control and more emphasis on code review than Git-based tools do.

## Features:

**Phabricator:** A number of tools for managing projects, tracking bugs, and conducting code reviews are included in

Phabricator. Inline comments, review requests, and automated linting are supported by its Differential code review tool.

- **Features:** Phabricator is a full-featured tool suite that combines issue tracking, project management, and code review into one cohesive picture of development progress.
- **Equation using Tools Based on Git:** Although Phabricator has a wider range of tools than Git-based solutions with more specialized code review features, this increased versatility could also come with additional complexity.

## Main Features and Advantages

- **Independence from Version Control:** Standalone solutions can interface with several versions of the version control system (VCS) and provide flexibility for teams employing different VCS alternatives.
- **Customization:** These technologies frequently offer a wide range of customization choices for user interfaces, workflows, and review procedures.
- **Specialized Features:** They concentrate on offering

sophisticated features for code reviews, like configurable dashboards, in-depth metrics, and interfaces with additional development tools.

## Difference with Tools Based on Git

- **Integration:** While Git-based tools come with built-in integration with Git, standalone tools could need further setup to work with version control systems.
- **Feature Set:** Unlike Git-based solutions, standalone tools frequently include specific functionality for code review that might not be as well-integrated with version control procedures.
- **Intricacy:** Because they have different integration needs and larger feature sets, standalone tools may add more complexity.

## 5.3 Code Review Tools in the Cloud

## Cloud-Based Solutions

The benefits of using cloud-based code review tools

include scalability, accessibility, and integration with other cloud-based development tools.

## Features:

- **Crucible:** Crucible has code review features like threaded conversations, inline comments, and version control system integration. It offers thorough review metrics and facilitates review workflows.

- **Perks:** Crucible is a cloud-based solution that can be scaled and accessed from any location, which makes it ideal for remote teams. To improve project management, it also interfaces with other Atlassian products, like Jira.

- **Equation using Tools Based on Git:** Although Crucible's cloud-based architecture allows for flexibility and scalability, certain of the integrated version control integrations that are present in Git-based solutions might not be present.

## Upsource:

- **Features:** Upsource provides JetBrains development tool integration, code review, and repository browsing. It offers a consistent review interface, code analytics, and support for inline comments.

- **Perks:** Development workflows are improved by Upsource's interaction with JetBrains tools, and its cloud-based deployment provides scalability and accessibility.

- **Equation using Tools Based on Git:** Although Upsource has strong review capabilities, depending on the particular version control system being used, it could not be as Git-integrated as Git-based applications.

## Benefits of Cloud-Based Technologies

- **Accessibility:** Cloud-based solutions enable dispersed and remote teamwork since they can be accessed from any internet-connected device.

- **Scalability:** Cloud solutions, which provide flexible consumption and storage options, may readily grow with team size and project complexity.

- **Automatic Updates:** Cloud-based solutions get maintenance and updates automatically, relieving internal IT personnel of some of the work and guaranteeing access to the newest features and security fixes.

## Combining with Additional Development Tools

- **Development Ecosystem:** A variety of development tools, such as CI/CD pipelines, issue tracking systems, and project management software, are frequently integrated with cloud-based code review tools.

- **Streamlined Workflows:** By integrating with other cloud-based applications, a development workflow can be made more efficient and collaborative throughout all stages of the process.

- **Data Synchronization:** Cloud-based solutions enable real-time synchronization with other tools, guaranteeing that team members can examine comments and see the most recent code modifications.

Teams can investigate standalone, cloud-based, and Git-based code review tools to choose the one that best suits their requirements. They can take into account features, workflow compatibility, and integration with version control systems. Teams may optimize their code review procedures and raise the overall quality of their code by taking advantage of the distinct benefits and considerations that each tool type offers.

# CHAPTER 6

## GitHub's Deep Dive into Code Review Tools

## 6.1 Features of GitHub's Code Review

## Requests in Bulk and the Code Review Procedure

**Requests for Pulls:**

- **Definition:** One GitHub tool that makes it easier to propose changes to a codebase is the pull request (PR). To start a review process for their code modifications before integrating them into the main branch, developers submit pull requests.

- **Workflow:** GitHub shows a comparison of the changes between the base branch and the suggested branch when a pull request is issued. Reviewers have the option to accept or reject the pull request, make changes requests, and offer comments on individual lines.

- **Merger Techniques:** GitHub provides a range of

merging techniques, such as rebasing, squashing commits, and merge commits. These tactics support the team's preferred workflow and aid in keeping a tidy commit history.

## Code Review Process:

- **Review Workflow:** There are usually multiple steps in the review process:
- **Generating a Pull Request:** After making modifications, developers submit a pull request.
- **Code Review:** Reviewers examine the code, offer criticism, and recommend modifications.
- **Addressing Feedback:** Based on reviewer comments, the author makes changes to the code.
- **Approval and Merging:** The pull request is accepted and merged into the base branch when the code satisfies the necessary requirements.
- **Examine Measures:** Metrics like time to first review, time to merge, and number of comments are available on GitHub and can be used to evaluate how effective and efficient the code review process is.

# Integrations and Collaboration Tools

## Inline Remarks:

- **Functionality:** Reviewers are able to directly comment on individual lines of the pull request code. Feedback that is exact and context-specific is made possible by this feature.
- **Apply:** You can point out problems, make suggestions for enhancements, and pose inquiries on the code changes using inline comments.

## Requests for Reviews:

- **Availability:** To make sure that the appropriate individuals are participating in the review process, authors have the option to seek reviews from particular teams or members.
- **Apply:** Review requests aid in workload management and guarantee that modifications are examined by appropriate or knowledgeable parties.

## Integrations:

- **CI/CD Integration:** To automate testing and

deployment, GitHub connects with a number of continuous integration and continuous deployment (CI/CD) technologies, including GitHub Actions, Travis CI, and CircleCI.

- **Issue Tracking Integration:** Pull requests can be easily linked to relevant issues or tasks thanks to GitHub's integration with issue tracking software like Jira.

- **Independent Resources:** Code quality checkers and security scanners are just two examples of the third-party apps and integrations available in GitHub's Marketplace that improve code review capabilities.

## Optimal Methods for Conducting Code Reviews on GitHub

- **Set Up Branch Protection Rules:** Establish branch protection rules to make sure that all modifications adhere to the team's quality standards by enforcing conditions such code review approvals prior to merging.

- **Define Review Guidelines:** Clearly state what is

expected of you in terms of feedback, approval standards, and response timeframes for code reviews.

- **Use Labels and Tags:** Use labels and tags to prioritize reviews, classify pull requests, and monitor the progress of code changes.
- **Make Use of GitHub Actions:** Use GitHub Actions to automate code review procedures in order to run tests, evaluate the quality of the code, and enforce coding standards.

## 6.2 GitHub's Advanced Code Review Methods

### Required Reviews and Code Owners

### Definition:

- **Code Owners:** Code owners are people or groups in charge of particular sections of the codebase. They are listed in a GitHub repository's `CODEOWNERS` file.
- **Application:** To make sure that modifications are reviewed by professionals who are familiar with the code, code owners are automatically asked to review

pull requests that have an impact on the code areas they own.

## Required Reviews:

- **Definition:** A branch protection feature that mandates certain reviews be completed before modifications are merged is called required reviews.
- **Configured as follows**: To make sure that a pull request needs a specific amount of approvals or reviews from approved code owners before it can be merged, repository administrators can set up necessary reviews.

## Regulations for Branch Protection

## Purpose:

- By imposing particular constraints and limitations on pull requests, branch protection rules aid in preserving the integrity of significant branches (such as `main} and `develop}).

## Setup:

- **Necessary Status Verifications:** Make sure pull

requests pass automated tests and verifications prior to merging.

- **Require Reviews for Pull Requests:** Make it mandatory for pull requests to be examined and accepted by one or more reviewers prior to merging.

- **Restrict Who Can Push:** Grant only particular users or teams the authority to push changes directly to protected branches.

## Automated Checks and Code Review

**Automated Verifications:**

- **Information**: Tests or analyses that are performed automatically as a part of the pull request procedure are known as automated checks. Linting, security scanning, and unit tests are a few examples of these.

- **Configured as follows:** Integrated CI/CD tools or GitHub Actions can be used to configure automated checks. They guarantee code quality and assist in identifying problems early in the development process.

## Configuring GitHub Actions:

- **Workflows:** Establish workflows to automate code construction, testing, and deployment, among other code review phases.

- **Custom Actions:** Apply custom actions, such applying coding standards or running static analysis tools, to customize automated checks to the particular requirements of the project.

## 6.3 GitHub Code Review Tips to Help You Work Effectively

### Writing Intense and Useful Criticism

### Be Specific:

- **Detail:** Offer thorough input on particular lines of code or areas that want improvement. Keep your remarks clear to avoid confusing others.

- **Instances:** Give examples or brief snippets of code to support your arguments and offer possible fixes.

## Be Constructive:

- **Focus on the Code:** Consider the code itself while providing input, not the skills of the author. Rather than critiquing the individual, try to improve the codebase.

- **Provide Options:** When highlighting problems, make recommendations for different strategies or fixes to aid the author in understanding how to handle the issue.

## Act Professionally:

- **Speech:** Deliver all feedback in a courteous and professional manner. Make sure your remarks are succinct, straightforward, and devoid of insults directed towards you.

- **Encouragement:** Provide constructive criticism in addition to positive reinforcement for well-written code and improvements accomplished.

## Avoiding Disagreements and Combining Pull Requests

## Resolve Conflicts

- **Merge Issues:** Resolve merge issues that could occur when combining code modifications from various branches. To settle disputes before submitting updates, use GitHub's dispute resolution tools or find an alternative locally.

- **Interaction:** Engage in dialogue with team members to comprehend the background of conflicting modifications and work out solutions that support the project's objectives.

**Merging Pull Requests:**

- **Approval:** Prior to merging a pull request, make sure that all necessary approvals and reviews have been obtained.

- **merging Strategies:** Based on the project's workflow and the type of changes, select the best merging strategy (such as merge commit, squash, or rebase).

- **Post-Merge Actions:** Following the merge, keep an eye on how the changes are integrating and take care of any problems that come up during testing or deployment.

## Improving Code Quality with Code Review

### Identify Patterns:

- **Common Issues**: Utilize code review input to find patterns or recurrent problems in the codebase, including frequent defects or inconsistencies in the coding style.

- **Training Opportunities:** To avoid recurring difficulties, update coding standards or provide team training to address prevalent concerns.

### Ongoing Enhancement:

- **Review Loop:** Create a feedback loop in which the insights from code reviews are used to the ongoing improvement of coding procedures, instruments, and workflows.

- **Best Practices:** To improve the general quality and maintainability of the code, encourage adherence to best practices and coding standards.

Teams may efficiently manage their code review procedures, foster collaboration, and produce higher-quality code by utilizing GitHub's code review features, cutting-edge methods, and best practices. GitHub offers a strong code review platform that works well with various development tools and workflows, assisting teams in upholding strict code quality standards.

# CHAPTER 7

GitLab, a Deep Dive into Code Review Tools

## 7.1 GitLab's Features for Code Reviews

### Workflow for Code Reviews and Merge Requests

**Requests for Merge (MRs):**

- **Explanation:** A GitLab tool called a Merge Request (MR) enables developers to suggest modifications to the codebase. MRs serve the same purpose as pull requests on GitHub: they are used for code review, discussion, and integration.

**Workflow:**

- **Establishing an MR:** In order to suggest changes, developers submit an MR. A summary of the modifications, a comparison of the code variations, and a commenting feature are all included in the MR.

- **Examining and Talking About**: Reviewers offer

suggestions and comments on the MR as feedback. Prior to approving the MR, they may propose modifications.

- **Approving and Combining:** The MR can be merged into the target branch once it has obtained the required approvals. Various merge techniques, including fast-forward merges, squashing commits, and merging commits, are supported by GitLab.

## Workflow for Code Reviews:

- **MR Creation and Assignment:** Based on their expertise or the needs of the project, authors write MRs and allocate them to reviewers.

- **Review Process:** Reviewers examine the code updates, offer feedback, and ask for adjustments as needed. GitLab facilitates threaded discussions and inline comments.

- **Automated Checks:** As part of the MR process, GitLab may be set up to do automated tests and checks, guaranteeing code quality and standard compliance.

- **Completing MRs:** The MR is authorized after taking into account the input, and any merge requirements are satisfied before merging into the main branch.

## Using CI/CD Pipelines for Integration

### Constant Integration (CI):

- **Explanation:** CI is the process of automatically generating and testing code modifications to make sure they work properly with the current codebase.

- **Using MRs in Integration**: GitLab automatically builds apps, runs tests, and verifies code changes as part of the review process by integrating CI pipelines with MRs. This guarantees that code satisfies quality requirements prior to merging and aids in the early detection of errors.

### Continuous Deployment (CD):

- **Definition:** CD (continuous deployment) automates the deployment of code updates to production or staging environments.

- **Using MRs in Integration:** GitLab may streamline the deployment process by eliminating manual processes by automating deployments based on merge events or MR approvals.

## Features of Code Quality

## Code Quality Reports:

- **Definition:** GitLab offers tools for code quality analysis and report generation, emphasizing problems like complexity, style infractions, and code smells.

- **Apply:** Reviewers can notice possible problems and make sure that code complies with quality requirements before merging thanks to the integration of code quality reports into MRs.

## Analysis, both static and dynamic:

- **Analysis, static:** Static analysis tools can be used with GitLab to examine code without running it. This aids in the detection of problems like code smells and security flaws.

- **Analytical Overview:** GitLab facilitates the use of dynamic analysis tools, which identify runtime problems and performance bottlenecks by conducting tests and checks while the code is running.

## 7.2 Using GitLab for Advanced Code Review

### Approvals for Code Reviews and Merge Conditions

### Code Review Approvals:
- **Definition:** GitLab enables the setup of approval rules, which mandate a predetermined quantity or kind of approvals prior to the merging of an MR.
- Configured as follows: Administrators can establish approval rules according to the quantity of necessary approvals, the approval of specified teams, or the approval of particular approvers.

### Merge Conditions:
- **Definition:** Merge conditions are requirements that must be fulfilled, including passing code quality standards or automating tests, in order for an MR to be merged.
- Configured as follows: Requirements such as successful CI/CD pipeline runs, approvals for code reviews, and compliance with branch protection

policies can be included in merge conditions.

## Security Checks and Vulnerability Scanning

## Scan for Vulnerabilities:

- **Definition:** GitLab has built-in security tools to check code for flaws and security problems.

## The following are some examples of scan types:

- **Static Application Security Testing (SAST):** Examines code for security flaws without running it.
- **Dynamic Application Security Testing (DAST):** uses attack simulation to test apps in use for security flaws.

## Integrated Security Checks:

- **Procedure:** Before code is merged, security checks are incorporated into the CI/CD pipeline and executed automatically as part of the MR process to find and fix security concerns.

## Personalizing the Procedure for Code Review

### Personalized Review Guidelines:

- **Introduction:** GitLab enables the code review procedure to be customized by specifying rules and procedures that are suited to the requirements of the project or company.

### Instances:

- **Rules for Custom Approval:** Set up the approval requirements according to the demands of the project; for example, require approvals from teams or roles in particular.

- **Examine the templates:** To standardize the review process, create templates for MR descriptions and review comments.

### Automated Workflows:

- **Definition:**Use GitLab's API and CI/CD pipelines to automate tedious chores and standardize review procedures.

### Examples include:

- **Automated Testing:** Set up pipelines to do quality

checks and tests automatically.

- **Check Out The Reminders:** Automated reminders for awaiting approvals or reviews can be set up.

## 7.3 GitLab Code Review Best Practices

## Offering Helpful Criticism

## Explain in Detail:

- **Be Particular:** Give specific code lines or parts your full criticism. Clearly state the need for adjustments and make recommendations for enhancements.
- **Instances:** Make sure your criticism is actionable by illustrating your points with code snippets or references.

## Show Constructiveness:

- **Pay Attention to Improvement:** Present criticism in a way that promotes development and education. Steer clear of personal attacks and concentrate on the code itself.
- **Provide Remedies:** When pointing out problems, provide answers or substitutes to enable the writer to

properly respond to the criticism.

## Act Professionally:

- **Speech:** Deliver all feedback in a courteous and professional manner. Make sure your remarks are succinct, precise, and devoid of offensive language.
- **Encouragement:** Offer constructive criticism in addition to positive reinforcement by praising well-written code or advancements made.

## Effective Process for Code Review

## Establish Review Guidelines:

- **Definition:** Clearly define the parameters and requirements for the code review procedure, including standards for approvals, response times, and the caliber of input.
- **Documentation:** To guarantee uniformity and adherence, document review guidelines and make them available to all team members.

## Review Process Streamlining:

- **Automate Repetitive chores:** Make use of GitLab's

automation features to manage merge requests and run tests, among other repetitive chores.

- **Ranking of Reviews:** Establish a mechanism for ranking reviews according to their influence on the project, urgency, or complexity of the code.

## Monitor and Improve:

- **Review data:** Keep track of data like the amount of comments, review turnaround times, and time to review in order to gauge how effective the code review process is.
- **Ongoing Enhancement:** In order to continuously enhance the review process and handle any bottlenecks or difficulties that may develop, use the feedback and data from code reviews.

## Taking Advantage of GitLab's Features to Boost Code Quality

## Make Use of Code Quality Reports:

- **Integration:** Include code quality reports in the MR process to identify problems and guarantee that the code satisfies quality requirements prior to merging.

- **fix Issues:** Examine code quality reports to fix problems like complexity, odors in the code, and stylistic inconsistencies.

## Automated Checks Implementation

- **CI/CD Pipelines:** Set up CI/CD pipelines to perform code quality checks, security scans, and automated tests as part of the MR process.
- **Custom Checks:** Create custom checks or automate extra quality assurance tasks based on the requirements of the project using GitLab's API.

## Promote Best Practices:

- **Standardize Code Practices:** By incorporating tools and guidelines into the code review process, encourage adherence to coding standards and best practices.
- **Promote Education:** Take advantage of code reviews to exchange best practices and information, encouraging a culture of learning and constant growth among team members.

Teams may improve their code review procedures,

collaborate better, and maintain high standards of code quality by utilizing GitLab's code review tools, advanced methodologies, and best practices. GitLab's extensive feature set facilitates successful software development and delivery by enabling efficient and productive code reviews.

# CHAPTER 8

## BITBUCKET: A COMPREHENSIVE CODE REVIEW TOOL

## 8.1 Bitbucket's Functionality for Code Reviews

## Requests in Bulk and the Code Review Procedure

**Requests for Pulls:**

- **Definition:** A Pull Request (PR) on Bitbucket is a request to combine changes from one branch into another. Code reviews and discussions can take place prior to changes being merged into the target branch.

**Workflow:**

- **Generating a Pull Request:** By choosing the source and destination branches, developers generate a PR. A summary of the modifications, pertinent code diffs, and a commenting feature are all included in the PR.

- **Examination and Comments:** Reviewers look over

the code changes, make comments, and ask for adjustments as needed. To make thorough evaluations easier, Bitbucket offers threaded discussions and inline comments.

- **Approving and Combining:** The PR can be merged into the target branch after it has been examined and approved. Bitbucket offers a variety of merging procedures, such as rebasing, squashing, and merge commits.

## Code Review Workflow:

- **Starting a Review:** Writers generate a pull request (PR) and designate reviewers, naming specific people or groups to examine the changes.
- **Reviewing Changes:** Reviewers examine the code modifications, offer comments, and ask for any adjustments that are required. Bitbucket's interface makes it possible to examine and debate code in detail.
- **Automated Checks:** As part of the PR process, Bitbucket connects with CI/CD pipelines to execute automated tests and checks, guaranteeing the quality of the code before merging.

## Jira with Trello Integration

### Jira Integration:

- **Problems with Linking:** Developers can link Jira issues to PRs by integrating Bitbucket with Jira. This linking helps track progress toward particular tasks or defects and gives context for the changes.

- **Updates Automatically**: Project management and tracking are streamlined via integration, which permits automatic updates of Jira issues depending on PR status, comments, and merging events.

### Card Linking:

- **Trello Integration:** Developers can attach pull requests (PRs) to Trello cards by using Bitbucket's integration with Trello. With this integration, you can keep tabs on code modifications and evaluate your progress toward particular goals or features.

- **Updates Automatically:** Updates on Trello cards can be triggered by changes in Bitbucket, which helps to maintain project management tools current with development activities.

## Features for Code Collaboration

## Definition:

- **Inline Comments:** Reviewers can directly comment on individual lines of code with Bitbucket's support for inline commenting on code diffs.
- **Apply:** Reviewers have the ability to annotate code, highlight specific changes, and start conversations about those modifications.

## Threaded Discussions:

- **Definition:** Bitbucket has a threaded discussion feature that enables structured discussions over code modifications.
- **Advantages:** Threaded chats make it easier to track review talks and decisions by keeping input relevant and organized.

## Code Review Checklist:

- **Definition:** Bitbucket allows checklists to be created inside of PRs, assisting in making sure that all relevant review requirements are met.

- **Apply:** Items like code style compliance, testing requirements, and documentation updates can all be found on checklists.

## 8.2 Bitbucket Advanced Code Review

### Branch Authorizations and Limitations

### Branch Permissions:

- **Definition:** Bitbucket allows you to choose who can merge code into protected branches, push changes, and initiate pull requests.
- **Configured as follows:** To guarantee that only authorized users are able to make modifications to crucial branches, permissions can be configured either at the repository or branch level.

### Restrictions:

- **Merge Restrictions:** Establish guidelines to limit merges according to standards like the quantity of approvals needed or the state of automated testing.
- **Code Review Requirements:** Establish guidelines mandating code reviews prior to merging

modifications in order to preserve consistency and quality of the code.

## Code Coverage and Insights

### Code Insights:

- **Definition:** Bitbucket offers metrics like code complexity, code churn, and review history to help users get insight into code changes.
- **Apply:** Throughout the review process, code insights assist reviewers in understanding the effects of modifications and making well-informed recommendations.

### Code Coverage:

- **Definition:** Bitbucket provides metrics on test coverage for modifications by integrating with code coverage tools.
- **Apply:** Reports on code coverage are useful in locating untested code and ensuring that modifications do not adversely affect test coverage.

## Personalizing the Process of Code Review

### Custom Review Rules:

- **Definition:** Bitbucket enables rules and parameters that are customized to the requirements of the project to be used in review processes.

### Instances:

- **Rules of Approval:** Establish guidelines for the quantity and kind of approvals needed before a merger.
- Examine the templates: To standardize the review process, create templates for PR descriptions and review comments.

### Automation and Integration:

- **Definition**: Automate code review process steps like starting automated tests or updating external tools by utilizing Bitbucket's API and integrations.

### Instances:

- **Custom Workflows:** Put in place automated workflows to manage policies for reviews or to handle repetitive chores.

- **Integration with Third-Party Tools:** Include other tools, like security scanners or code quality analyzers, to improve the review procedure.

## 8.3 Bitbucket Code Review Tips to Help You Write Better Code

### Writing Brief and Explicit Remarks

### Be Specific:

- **Definition:** Give detailed comments on certain lines of code segments. Clearly state the problems and offer solutions.
- **Instances:** Make sure your comments are pertinent and actionable, and include code samples to demonstrate your arguments.

### Be Constructive:

- **Focus on Code:** Present feedback in a way that prioritizes enhancement of the code over subjective criticism. Make helpful ideas and draw attention to the code's advantages.
- **Encouragement:** Give writers credit for

well-executed features or enhancements.

## Make Explicit:

- **Vernacular:** When leaving comments, use language that is simple and unambiguous. Steer clear of jargon and unclear terminology that can cause miscommunication.
- **Arrangement:** When organizing feedback, use numbered lists or bullet points to make comments easier to understand.

## Mentoring Team Members Through Code Review

## Guidance:

- **Mentorship:** Take use of code reviews to mentor team members by imparting best practices, coding conventions, and design patterns.
- **Teaching Moments:** Point out areas in which developers may strengthen their abilities and offer clarifications or additional resources to support them.

## Promote Learning:

- **Response:** Provide feedback that promotes development and learning. Give justifications for the recommendations made and the ways in which they improve the quality of the code.

- **Sources:** Provide team members with links to pertinent guides, instructions, or resources that can help them become more proficient coders.

## Optimizing the Procedure for Code Review

## Define Clear Guidelines:

- **Guidelines:** Specify expectations and guidelines for the code review procedure, such as standards for approvals, response times, and the caliber of input.

- **Documentation:** To guarantee uniformity and adherence, document policies and make them available to every team member.

## Automate Repetitive Tasks:

- **Automation:** Make use of Bitbucket's automation tools to automate repetitive processes, such handling pull requests and running automated tests.

- **Integration:** Automate code quality checks and expedite the review process by integrating with CI/CD technologies.

**Streamline Workflow:**

- **Prioritization:** Establish a method to rank PRs according to their influence on the project, code complexity, or urgency.
- **Efficiency:** Keep an eye on and evaluate the code review procedure on a regular basis to spot potential areas for enhancement and streamline procedures for increased effectiveness.

Through the utilization of Bitbucket's sophisticated methods, best practices, and code review features, teams may optimize their code review procedures, foster better teamwork, and uphold superior code quality standards. Bitbucket's extensive feature set facilitates successful software development and delivery by enabling efficient and effective code reviews.

# CHAPTER 9

REVIEW BOARD DEEP DIVE AS A CODE REVIEW TOOL

## 9.1 Overview of the Review Board

## Principles and Advantages

## Code Review Interface:

- **Overview:** Review Board offers a web-based code review interface. With possibilities for inline comments and threaded discussions, it facilitates the transparent and structured assessment of modifications.

- **Benefits:** Facilitates feedback and teamwork by providing an easy-to-use interface for browsing and discussing code changes, hence improving the review process.

**Overview:**

- **Diff Viewing:** Users can examine differences between code revisions inline or side by side using the Review Board. This feature aids reviewers in comprehending the modifications made in relation to earlier iterations.

- **Features:** The efficiency of the review process is increased by the ability to more easily identify changes and potential problems with side-by-side comparisons and inline diffs.

**Commenting and Discussion:**

- **Overview:** Inline commenting is supported by the Review Board, enabling reviewers to directly comment on individual lines of code. It also facilitates threaded discussions for structured dialogue over code modifications.

- **Features:** While threaded discussions aid in maintaining the organization and focus of review talks, inline comments offer context-specific criticism.

## Approval procedure:

- **Overview:** The Review Board has capabilities to manage the code review approval procedure, such as choices for assigning reviewers and necessary approvals.

- **Benefits:** Ensures that code modifications are examined and authorized by relevant stakeholders prior to integration, streamlining the review process.

## Version Control System Integration

## Supported Systems:

- **Overview:** Git, Subversion (SVN), and Mercurial are just a few of the version control systems (VCS) that Review Board interfaces with. Code review procedures can now be carried out smoothly inside the framework of current version control procedures thanks to this integration.

- **Advantages:** Makes code modifications easier to retrieve and incorporates code review procedures into current workflows.

**Overview:**

- **Repository Integration:** Review Board automatically retrieves and displays code changes for review by establishing direct connections to version control repositories. Through the removal of manual procedures, this integration streamlines the review process.

- **Advantages:** Reduces administrative overhead by automating the retrieval and display of code changes, streamlining the code review process.

**Automated Updates:**

- **Overview:** Review Board has the ability to send out notifications and automatically update code review statuses in response to modifications made to the version control system.

- **Features:** ensures quick feedback and decision-making by keeping all stakeholders updated on the most recent advancements and modifications to the code review procedure.

## Personalized Process

## Custom Workflows:

- **Overview:** The Review Board enables the review workflow to be tailored to the particular requirements of the company. This entails establishing unique permission procedures, notifications, and review phases.
- **Features:** makes adjustments to the review procedure to bring it into compliance with company standards and procedures, increasing efficiency.

## Review Templates:

- **Overview:** To standardize the review process, users can design and apply custom review templates. Pre-established checklists and reviewer standards are examples of templates.
- **Features:** maintains high standards across various projects and teams and guarantees consistency in the review process.

## 9.2 Review Board for Advanced Code Review

## Discernible Evaluations and Side-by-Side Analyses

### Overview:

- **Review Board offers the ability for Differential Reviews:** Reviewers can compare several code revisions to comprehend changes and their effects.
- **Features:** allows for a thorough analysis of code alterations, making it easier to spot problems and judge the quality of changes.

### Comparing Side by Side:

- **Overview:** The program allows for side-by-side diff views, which arrange the differences between two code versions to be seen side by side. This feature improves comprehension of code updates and readability.
- **Features:** simplifies the process of identifying code version discrepancies and evaluating the effects of modifications.

# Policies and Templates for Code Reviews

## Code Review Policies:

- **Overview:** Review Board gives businesses the ability to specify and implement code review guidelines, such as approval procedures, reviewer assignments, and review completion standards.

- **Advantages:** Promotes uniformity and quality by guaranteeing that code reviews follow organizational standards and procedures.

## Overview:

- **Review Templates:** It is possible to add particular review criteria, checklists, and guidelines to code review templates. Templates guarantee thorough evaluations and help standardize the review procedure.

- **Benefits:** Provides an organized method and guarantees that all relevant review components are covered, streamlining the review process.

## Analysis and Reporting

### Overview:

- Review Board provides analytics and reporting tools to monitor important code review metrics like approval rates, review turnaround times, and review comments.
- **Benefits:** Helps pinpoint areas in need of development by offering insights into the efficacy and efficiency of the code review process.

### Personalized Reports:

- **Oversight:** Users are able to create personalized reports according to particular standards or data that pertain to their review procedures. It is possible to customize reports to satisfy the requirements of various stakeholders.
- **Advantages:** Provides companies with the ability to monitor and evaluate performance in a manner that corresponds with their particular needs and goals.

## 9.3 Review Board Usage Best Practices

### Setup of an Effective Code Review Process

### Define Specific Goals:

- **Overview:** Specify specific goals for the code review process, such as those pertaining to knowledge sharing, coding standard observance, and code quality.
- **Benefits:** Ensures that each participant is aware of the review's goal and expectations.

### Establish Review rules:

- **Overview**: Create and record rules for carrying out code reviews, including with standards for feedback needs, review completeness, and code quality.
- **Features:** gives code reviews a defined method that encourages thoroughness and uniformity.

### Train Authors and Reviewers:

- **Overview:** Train reviewers and code writers on efficient code review procedures, how to utilize

Review Board capabilities, and appropriate ways to provide and receive criticism.

- **Benefits:** Ensures that all participants are knowledgeable and proficient, which improves the review process's overall efficacy.

## Encouraging Participation in Code Reviews

### Cultivate a Collaborative Culture:

- **Overview:** Establish a setting where teamwork is valued and encouraged when doing code reviews. Encourage a culture that values ongoing development and helpful criticism.
- **Benefits:** Promotes a positive and effective review environment and raises participation in the review process.

### Recognize work:

- **Overview**: Thank reviewers and code writers for their work. Formal awards, shout-outs during team meetings, and other kinds of acknowledgment can all be used as forms of recognition.
- **Advantages:** Encourages participation in the

evaluation process and cultivates a sense of pride and ownership in the work.

## Using Review Boards to Exchange Knowledge

### Document Review Insights:

- **Overview:** Make use of Review Board's functionality to record and distribute code review insights, like common problems, recommended practices, and lessons discovered.

- **Advantages:** Encourages knowledge exchange and aids in creating a database of important data that team members can consult.

### Support Conversations:

- **Overview:** Promote dialogue and information exchange using the Review Board's comment and discussion tools. Utilize these conversations to debate issues, exchange knowledge, and work together to find answers.

- **Features:** increases team members' knowledge base and facilitates learning from one another's experiences and skills.

Teams may boost communication, maintain high standards of code quality, and improve their code review processes by utilizing Review Board's advanced capabilities and adhering to best practices. The strong capabilities of the Review Board facilitate successful and efficient code reviews, which aid in software creation and ongoing enhancement.

# CHAPTER 10

## PHABRICATOR: A DEEP DIVE INTO CODE REVIEW TOOLS

## 10.1 Features of Phabricator's Code Review

## Differential Approach to Code Review and Revision

### Differential Edits:

- **Summary:** The main tool for code review in Phabricator's Differential. It has an extensive interface that lets users submit, examine, and keep track of code modifications.

- **Workflow:** Phabricator provides a clean and well-organized presentation of changes when a developer submits a divergent revision. Before the code is accepted, reviewers have the ability to make comments on individual lines, offer suggestions, and ask for changes.

- **Features:** ensures that all feedback is recorded and taken into consideration by providing code modifications and comments in an intuitive manner, hence facilitating an organized code review process.

## Review Workflow:

- **Overview:** Phabricator's review process consists of multiple steps, such as submission, review, commenting, and approval. Every step is made to guarantee that code modifications are thoroughly examined and discussed.

- **Workflow:** Code changes are submitted by developers as differential revisions, which are subsequently examined by assigned reviewers. Reviewers offer comments, make adjustments requests, and finally decide whether to accept or reject the revision based on its quality and adherence to criteria.

- **Features:** A structured approach guarantees that all modifications are approved before integration and aids in maintaining high code quality.

## Combining with Additional Development Tools

- **Overview:** Phabricator interfaces with a number of

version control systems (VCS), including Git, Mercurial, and Subversion. Code changes may be seamlessly linked to the review process thanks to this connectivity.

- **Benefits:** Makes it easier to follow changes and debates by automatically linking code modifications to their corresponding commits, simplifying the review process.

## Continuous Integration (CI) Tools:

- **Overview:** Utilizing CI tools in conjunction with Phabricator enables the automation of build and testing procedures. Code changes are tested prior to review thanks to this integration.
- **Features:** carries out automated tests and builds in tandem with code reviews to aid in the early identification and resolution of issues.

## Project Management Tools:

- **Overview:** Teams can associate code reviews with particular tasks, issues, or feature requests thanks to Phabricator's integration capabilities.
- **Features:** connects code changes to relevant tasks to

improve project tracking, increasing visibility and fostering better team cooperation among developers.

## Features of Collaboration and Communication

## Inline Comments:

- **Overview:** Within the differential revision, reviewers can leave inline comments on certain lines of code. This feature makes it easier to discuss code changes and provide thorough feedback.
- **Benefits:** Provides accurate and useful feedback, which facilitates addressing certain problems and raising the caliber of code.

## Threads for Discussion:

- **Overview:** Reviewers can have structured discussions over code changes with Phabricator's support for threaded discussions. Threads can be used to discuss problems, provide clarification, and work together to find answers.
- **Benefits:** Maintains concentration and organization during conversations, making sure that any criticism is noted and properly handled.

## Notifications and Alerts:

- **Overview:** Phabricator notifies stakeholders of updates and modifications to the review process through notifications and alerts. Users can personalize notifications according to their preferences.

- **Advantages:** Assures prompt correspondence and assists in keeping all parties informed about the progress of code evaluations.

## 10.2 Phabricator's Advanced Code Review

## Workflows and Policies for Code Reviews

## Workflows Customized:

- **Overview:** Review procedures can be tailored with Phabricator to meet the requirements of an organization. Steps in a workflow could include comprehensive analysis, ultimate approval, and preliminary review.

- **Features:** Optimizes the review procedure to conform to particular team protocols and demands, enhancing effectiveness and standard compliance.

## Review Policies:

- **Overview:** Teams can create and implement review policies in Phabricator, which can include acceptance criteria, review assignments, and approval requirements.
- **Benefits:** Boosts the caliber and dependability of the review process by ensuring that evaluations are carried out consistently and in accordance with organizational standards.

## Security checks and code audits

## Code Audits:

- **Overview:** Teams can inspect and evaluate code to see if it complies with security standards, best practices, and coding practices by using Phabricator's code audit tools.
- **Benefits:** Offers a methodical way to auditing code modifications, improving code quality and security.

## Security Checks:

- **Overview:** Automated security checks are made possible as part of the code review procedure by integration with security technologies. Security evaluations and vulnerability scans are included in this.

- **Advantages:** Lowers the possibility of vulnerabilities in the finished product by identifying and addressing security issues early in the development process.

## Personalizing Phabricator to Fit Your Group

## Custom Fields and Forms:

- **Overview:** Phabricator enables you to add custom attributes or requirements for differential changes to fields and forms used in the code review process.

- **Features:** modifies the review procedure to gather data pertinent to the unique requirements and procedures of your team.

**Automations and Integrations:**

- **Overview:** To improve functionality and expedite procedures, teams can integrate other tools with Phabricator and set up automations.

- **Features:** increases productivity by connecting with technologies that assist the development workflow and automating repetitive operations.

## 10.3 Phabricator Code Review Tips to Help You Write Better Code

### Offering Explicit and Helpful Feedback

**Be Specific:**

- **Overview:** When giving feedback, be clear about the problems or changes that need to be made. Make precise code references and give concise explanations.

- **Features:** aids writers in comprehending and appropriately responding to criticism, resulting in more successful and efficient edits.

## Be Constructive:

- **Overview:** Present criticism in a constructive way by emphasizing potential improvements rather than just listing flaws. If at all possible, provide recommendations or substitutes.

- **Benefits:** Promotes a cooperative approach to enhancing code quality and a favorable review experience.

## Using the Features of Phabricator to Increase Productivity

## Make Use of Inline Comments:

- **Overview:** Make use of inline comments to offer thorough criticism right in the context of the code modifications. Reviewers can target specific lines or sections with the use of this function.

- **Benefits:** Improves feedback's relevancy and clarity, making it simpler for writers to comprehend and apply changes.

## Make Use of Review Templates:

- **Overview:** Standardize the review process by creating and utilizing review templates. Checklists and requirements for various kinds of code reviews can be found in templates.

- **Advantages:** Assures uniformity in the evaluation procedure and aids in upholding high standards throughout various projects.

## Automate Routine Tasks:

- **Overview:** Configure Phabricator to do routine tasks, including alerting reviewers or changing review statuses, through automations.

- **Advantages:** Lessens manual labor and boosts management effectiveness for the review process.

## Building a Culture of Collaborative Code Reviews

## Encourage Open conversation:

- **Overview:** During code reviews, encourage courteous and open conversation. Invite team members to participate in conversations and offer their insights.

- **Advantages:** Promotes a cooperative atmosphere where discussions and feedback are welcomed and code quality is improved.

## Recognize work:

- **Overview:** Thank reviewers and code writers for their work. Both official and informal praise can be used to express recognition.
- **Advantages:** Encourages participation in the review process and fosters a supportive team environment.

Teams may maintain high standards of code quality, boost collaboration, and improve their code review processes by utilizing Phabricator's features and capabilities. The adaptability and sophisticated features of Phabricator facilitate successful software development and ongoing enhancement by enabling effective and efficient code reviews.

# ABOUT THE AUTHOR

 Author and thought leader in the IT field Taylor Royce is well known. He has a two-decade career and is an expert at tech trend analysis and forecasting, which enables a wide audience to understand complicated concepts.

Royce's considerable involvement in the IT industry stemmed from his passion with technology, which he developed during his computer science studies. He has extensive knowledge of the industry because of his experience in both software development and strategic consulting.

Known for his research and lucidity, he has written multiple best-selling books and contributed to esteemed tech periodicals. Translations of Royce's books throughout the world demonstrate his impact.

Royce is a well-known authority on emerging technologies and their effects on society, frequently requested as a speaker at international conferences and as a guest on tech podcasts. He promotes the development of ethical technology, emphasizing problems like data privacy and the digital divide.

In addition, with a focus on sustainable industry growth, Royce mentors upcoming tech experts and supports IT education projects. Taylor Royce is well known for his ability to combine analytical thinking with technical know-how. He sees a time when technology will ethically benefit humanity.

www.ingramcontent.com/pod-product-compliance
Lightning Source LLC
LaVergne TN
LVHW051657050326
832903LV00032B/3858